To my grandparents, for teaching me about gratitude, empathy and being mindful — thank you!

Happy Day Out in the Outback

Finn & Henry explore!

Author - Megan Carige
Illustrator - Honey Randall

KIDS TRAVEL GUIDE
Happy Day Out

Happy Day Out in the Outback
Author – Megan Carige

© Megan Carige 2019

www.happydayout.com.au
happydayoutbook@gmail.com

This book is sold with the understanding that the author is not offering specific personal advice to the reader. Although the author and illustrator have tried to make the information as accurate as possible, they accept no responsibility for any loss or risk, personal or otherwise, that happens as a consequence of the use and application of any of the contents of this book.

All rights reserved. This book may not be reproduced in whole or part, stored, posted on the internet, or transmitted in any form or by any means, electronic, mechanical, photocopying, recording, or other, except brief extracts for the purpose of review, without written permission from the author of this book.

Editing and publishing by: Alex Fullerton www.authorsupportservices.com
Illustrated by: Honey Randall

ISBN: 978-0-6483917-7-7

A catalogue record for this book is available from the National Library of Australia

Finn & Henry are two little boys,
who have for the moment
put away their toys.
They each have a map, they each have a pack;
they're off to explore the Aussie outback!

Queensland

The Charleville Cosmos Centre
with **huge** telescopes,
was very exciting, as we had hoped.
We saw the Southern Cross, the
Milky Way and hundreds of stars.
And look! Over there! We even saw Mars!

In Longreach at the Stockman's Hall of Fame,
we saw the olden times when
life was not the same.
The Qantas Founders Museum
with its history of flight;
sitting in those planes must have
been cramped and tight.

In Winton we did the Dinosaur
Trail and saw many bones;
we explored what's left of
these creatures' homes.
Waltzing Matilda Centre
tells of a special song,
about a swagman
sitting beside a billabong.

Northern Territory

The Northern Territory is part
of the vast top end,
where we fed big crocodiles
at the river bend.
We hiked around Kakadu National Park;
saw waterfalls and Aboriginal rock art.

Uluru is a huge rock; a visit here is a must.
We walked around it in the red, red dust.
It was such a long way for us,
we did our best.
But now it is time to take a big rest.

Western Australia

Next place to visit, the Kimberley Region,
with lots of emus, kangaroos
and camels even.
Kalgoorlie has a history of mining gold;
we looked around mines, new and old.

Oh look over there, a rock like a wave!
We pretended to surf then
found another fun cave.
We said goodbye to the West
and jumped on the train,
to travel across the Nullarbor Plain.

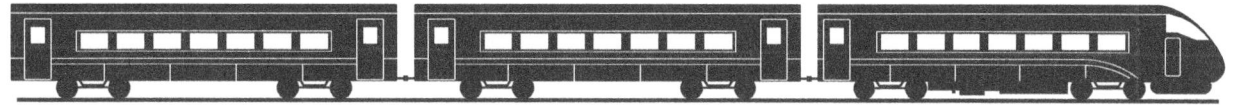

South Australia

Coober Pedy was full of gems to be found,
and we visited some homes
that were underground.
The Big Winch Lookout is up very high;
we looked out at the town, the
desert and the big blue sky.

Australia's lowest point is at Lake Eyre.
When filled with water there
are birds everywhere.
We saw galahs with feathers grey and pink.
The sun was so hot, we had
to put on our zinc.

Innamincka is a place to cruise
down the Cooper.
This inland river is really super.
Next we visited the famous Dig Tree.
The old carvings by explorers
were a sight to see.

New South Wales

We visited the Living Desert and
Sculptures in Broken Hill.
We were very busy; no time to stand still.
National Parks like Mungo and
Sturt we enjoyed some hikes,
sometimes we wished we had our bikes!

Our outback journey is nearing the end,
but there's one more place to recommend.
Lightning Ridge has so many things to do,
like opal mining and fossicking too.

Our Aussie outback journey
is one we love to share
So many things to see, if you dare.
Follow our footsteps as you read the book
Come on, get going and have a look....

Tick off the sites you visited with Finn & Henry...

☐ QLD:
Visit Charleville Cosmos Centre

☐ Visit the Stockman's Hall of Fame and Qantas Founders Museum in Longreach

☐ Explore the Dinosaur Trail and Waltzing Matilda Centre in Winton

☐ NT:
Feed big crocs and hike in Kakadu National Park

☐ Visit Uluru in central Australia

- [ ] **WA:** Visit the Kimberley and look for gold in Kalgoorlie

- [ ] Visit Wave Rock and pretend to surf

- [ ] **SA:** Look for homes underground in Coober Pedy

- [ ] Visit Lake Eyre

- [ ] Spot the Dig Tree

- [ ] **NSW:** Visit Broken Hill and hike in Mungo and Sturt National Parks

- [ ] Explore Lightning Ridge

About the Author

MEGAN CARIGE spent her earlier childhood living in Fiji before her family moved to Toowoomba in Queensland. Megan has spent most of her adult life living, working and visiting cities around Australia and the world.

Moving back to live in the beautiful Garden City of Toowoomba with her two young sons gave Megan the inspiration for her first children's story book, *Happy Day Out in Toowoomba*. She soon followed this with *Happy Day Out on the Sunshine Coast*.

Megan's third book, *Happy Day Out in the Outback* is now part of the successful Happy Day Out book series.

About the Illustrator

HONEY RANDALL is a Queensland girl through and through, and has lived in several locations around the Sunshine State. She enjoys drawing and writing, and works mostly digitally with the occasional piece using traditional pencils and pens.

Find more of her work at @honey_elizabeth_illustration on instagram

Also look out for:

 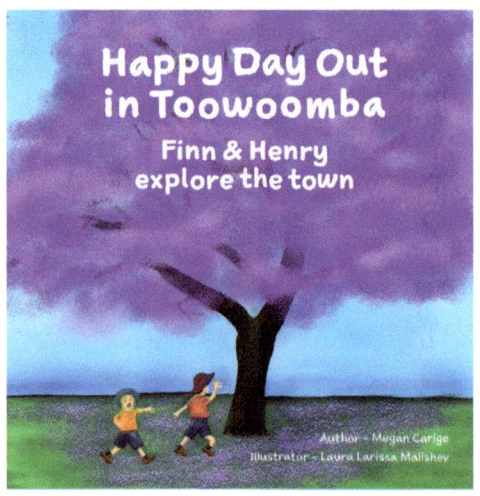

Happy Day Out on the Sunshine Coast

Happy Day Out in Toowoomba

Available at
www.happydayout.com.au

www.ingramcontent.com/pod-product-compliance
Lightning Source LLC
Chambersburg PA
CBHW061816290426
44110CB00026B/2889